T0066984

FISHING'S
BEST EXCUSES

FISHING'S BEST EXCUSES

Hilarious Quips Every Angler Should Know

Joshua Shifrin and Matt Mitchell

Skyhorse Publishing

Skyhorse Publishing books may be purchased in bulk at special discounts for sales promotion, corporate gifts, fund-raising, or educational purposes. Special editions can also be created to specifications. For details, contact the Special Sales Department, Skyhorse Publishing, 307 West 36th Street, 11th Floor, New York, NY 10018 or info@skyhorsepublishing.com.

Skyhorse® and Skyhorse Publishing® are registered trademarks of Skyhorse Publishing, Inc.®, a Delaware corporation.

Visit our website at www.skyhorsepublishing.com.

Please follow our publisher Tony Lyons on Instagram @tonylyonsisuncertain

10 9 8 7 6 5 4 3 2 1

Library of Congress Cataloging-in-Publication Data is available on file.

Cover design by Kai Texel
Cover artwork by Ian Baker

Print ISBN: 978-1-5107-7847-4
Ebook ISBN: 978-1-5107-7848-1

Printed in China

Introduction

Fishing! We ask you, is there anything better than spending a day on, over, next to, or in the water when the fish are really biting? Landing the big one, while basking under a sun-soaked sky, enjoying the day with some friends and a few of your favorite cold beverages, is time best spent.

From the days of our childhood fishing with our fathers and grandfathers, to currently taking our own children out on the open water, there is still little that invokes the same thrill as hooking into a fish and feeling the fight at the end of the line. The *tug* is the *drug*! At the end of the day, nothing compares to coming home with a full cooler, frying up your rewards, and playfully debating who had the biggest catch or reminiscing about the one that got away. Whether in a river up to our knees, on the shore, off a dock or bridge, or in a boat, we just love it all.

However, every angler worth his salt can tell you that there are days that just don't go according to plan. Even with the perfect equipment, the best bait, your favorite spot on the lake, and years of practice, there are going to be times when the fish just don't cooperate.

So, what is one to do? Sure, you could simply tell your hungry family and friends back home that it was beyond your control. Even with all your expertise, it was no hope. If Ishmael from *Moby Dick* himself was there to help, it wouldn't have mattered. The fish just weren't biting. Of course, there's a chance that your comrades will laugh and tell jokes at your expense, and as every good fisherman knows, this is completely unacceptable!

There's a good reason why anglers have been telling tall tales for years. Whether it's due to the poor weather, the bad bait, the unacceptable equipment, or simply because the fishing gods were out to get you, there's always a viable, or not so viable, excuse to explain your ineptitude.

So, the next time you come home with nothing to show for your efforts, there are countless reasons why your woeful performance couldn't possibly be your fault. Without further ado, we offer you, our friend, colleague, compatriot, a foolproof way to shed the blame, the embarrassment, the multitude of jokes at your expense. We give you, *Fishing's Best Excuses*.

The Excuses

IAN BAKER.

"I'm Against Fishing in the Rain!"

The days of "weather be damned" are not yet behind us. We will go to a football game and blister in the sun, freeze in a blizzard, and get soaked to the bone. But when it looks like it is going to rain on the lake—count us out! Whether summer storms or nasty frontal systems, the combination of rain and fishing is a valid and real excuse for a skunk. While the critical resource of water is necessary for all of our species to survive, for some reason we have not capitalized (most of us that is) on the ability to catch fish routinely and enjoy doing so . . . in the rain.

A great angler friend commonly says as a concession, "There are too many good days to fish on a day like today," as the heavens open, creating a blanket of dimples on the surface. We've sat in the truck at the boat ramp, wipers waving as we check the forecast, huddled under bridges, docks, and waterfront watering holes waiting out a storm. We'll roll over and get the best sleep of the year if the rain is dumping and giving us the ultimate excuse not to fish. But come Monday, we ramp up again for the mindset of "We will fish come hell or high water this weekend! Who's with us?"

"Is Wendy coming? This Wind is for Flying Kites, not Fishing!"

The most-watched forecast other than wedding days and Halloween are the days leading up to a fishing trip. It can be the bane of our existence, from wind knots, brutal wave action, and the lack of "feel" when you think you have casted to the perfect spot. A bow in your line curves to a giant "C" shape through the air on the surface of the unsettled water. With each day approaching, the forecast becomes further cemented and wind speed, gusts, or direction can hurt our chances and our egos. By inserting "Wendy" into the conversation as a new addition to the trip and a tip of the hat to the conditions we are stuck with, we can try to make light of the uncontrollable misery of a situation.

Many anglers discuss the upcoming fishing trip with friends in a wind code of sorts with friends by asking, "Is Wendy coming?" Meaning: Will that mean howl of gusting wind of misery give the fish the upper hand? More times than not, when Wendy arrives, the trip is primed nicely for an easy-out when the fishing trip turns to a boat ride, sunburned thighs, and a lost hat along the way. So, the next time you come home with an empty cooler, you can confidently state, "Wendy was to blame!"

"No Bait. (Oh Wait, Can We Eat That?)"

"This is our last cricket." Devastating words from the jon boat as the bluegill bite is on fire. Should've bought fifty more. Shouldn't have let those two slip away. Should've tried to use that dismembered one to catch another fish. We live and die by the bait on board. We tried to buy just enough but, damnit, we bought too many last trip, and had to feed them to the birds in the yard. Regionally, we use a variety of local "fish food," including live crickets, minners, shiners, greenies, shrimp, worms, goggle eye, eels, crabs, sand fleas, or your live bait of choice. Too much bait is never a problem when the bite is on, and pinpointing that perfect count of live bait to purchase only comes with good luck and experience.

If you've been fishing long enough, you will find out that you *never* want to run out of bait, therefore you tend to buy more than you could ever use. Some may call throwing a few extra bucks on the counter at the local bait and tackle shop "a cost of doing business" or "a risk not worth taking" with hopes to not leave the fish in a frenzy, and make more memories that will last a lifetime. As the fishing trip progresses, however, at some point there is a monumental shift in momentum and reality. Our stomachs begin to growl, sending a clear message to our brain. *What's for supper?* We couldn't let the bait die in vain! Chocolate-covered crickets or boiled minners, if we are hungry enough and haven't caught any keepers, are not ruled out.

Raise your hand if you've turned bait into table fare. A livewell overloaded with plump and juicy twelve-count shrimp starts to take on the pinkish-red hue of beautiful peel-and-eat shrimp on a plate with a pile of cocktail sauce on the side. Yes, we can eat that leftover bait . . . if we are hungry enough.

Did You Know?

Anglers might be interested to learn that the word "angle" comes from the Proto-Indo-European ancient language that means "hook."

"THROW THAT BANANA OVERBOARD NOW!"

Newbies, green horns, rookies, or other inexperienced anglers naturally have some nerves about going fishing. They want to be prepared for the day on the water and for reeling in the big one, which includes packing all of their creature comforts. They pack a cute little snack sack, a couple of drinks, and grab a banana. A BANANA! Absolutely not. No way. Bring canned sausages or leftover pizza but say no to the banana. The easiest way to chap off a seasoned angler and to ruin your chances of catching a single fish is by bringing a banana onboard.

A tall tale of fishy superstition dating back to the 1700s, when supposed shipwrecks were littered with floating bananas nearby, has scarred boat captains and anglers deeply. Simply put, for centuries the banana has been regarded as a key ingredient in the recipe for maritime disaster and is a no-no for all boating adventures—especially fishing. Newbies should know this: If your captain points this out quietly, get ready to catch some fish as they are not looking for an easy-out excuse for a lackluster fishing trip. If they double-down with an over-exaggerated showing, then your excuse-expert has been given their golden ticket to a skunk-fest of no fish . . . and you can let your mate know, "It's all because of you and your banana!"

"WE RAN AGROUND!"

"We're high and dry while the fish are chewing!"

Many channels are marked. Many are not. Some channels change with the season, while tides make navigation tricky and critically important. Running aground also has varying levels of criticality. We've been aboard, running wide open on the way out without a care in the world, and had that unmistakable simultaneous sound of the motor winding up while feeling a screeching halt. This is not a good feeling on the prettiest of days. It's much worse when it is very cold and there's a falling tide where depths will not return for hours.

You have now found yourself run hard aground on a day which has turned to a strong advantage of fish over man. Following channel markers (red / right return), your previous GPS tracks, or even other boats can help. As a last resort, in hopes of catching a fish, consider your options for wading to deeper waters while pondering your next move, but remember to throw out an anchor, albeit on dry land.

"My Hands Were Sweaty and I Dropped the Big One."

We like to fish in all weather. The cold, rain, wind, fog, you name it. But it goes without saying that nothing beats a beautiful, sun-soaked summer day. It may not happen often, but hear us out. The sun is overhead, the mercury in the thermometer continues to rise, and you're in a battle with a mammoth creature of the sea. Then, with the sweat pouring from your body, you finally reel it in. Unfortunately, when you are finally taking the hook out, the unthinkable happens. The large beast thrashes and you lose your grip only to watch your conquest escape back into the water. Upsetting? Well, yes. But there is a silver lining: you can embellish the story as you wish, only to end it with, "If my hands weren't so sweaty from such a mighty battle, I would be showing off my huge trophy right now!"

"Lockjaw—No Way They Bite in This Cold!"

Layer up—the excuses of cold weather are coming in thick. As a cold front approaches, fish begin their stingy and predictable preparations of disappointment for anglers. First the rain, thunder, and lightning blast through, followed by strong and gusty winds from the North, followed by bitter cold high-sky bluebird days. This, friends, is the most common set-up for "Lockjaw," or arguably the best excuse of all time for cold-weary and let-down anglers. You see, all of these weather events, including increased ultraviolet ray penetration into the water, are signals to fish that they are approaching a period of difficult times for feeding. A lockjaw pattern sets in, and fish oftentimes move to deeper, safer water and turn off the predatory instincts to bite.

This holding pattern will only subside when weather improves, which can take seven to ten days or longer. New techniques and baits such as lightweight, slow-moving presentations to get fish to bite during brutal post–cold front conditions have been studied extensively and are most commonly put into practice at major bass tournaments across the United States. Fact is that the number and size of fish caught reduces drastically. Lockjaw codes are still safe in deep waters and so is the fish's pointed advantage over the layered up and hopeful anglers above. "Cold as a well digger's ass out here is too cold for me to pretend like we are going to catch something!"

"THESE TIDES ARE NOT WORKING FOR US."

It's a negative low tide and we need two feet of water to fish.

The first tide machine was developed in 1872–73 by Sir William Thomson, and as a result tides can be continuously predicted and are published by the National Oceanic and Atmospheric Agency two years in advance. The trick, you see, is to line up this critically important variable with the other two most important dependencies: weather and availability to go fishing. When the tide doesn't "line up" you can expect the fishing to not either. This is one of the most valid excuses in the book.

It is, however, a very common excuse for a slow day on the water—whether the tide is too low, too high, or even "neaping," which is when there is the least difference between high and low tide, just after the first or third quarter phases of the moon. The tide can also be "ripping," meaning too much water is moving, or the common "we didn't have enough water moving"—both are also solid go-tos among guides and weekend anglers alike. Optimal feeding periods and chances of catching the most fish revolve around the tides and the time of the year. The best anglers find and catch fish when the tides "aren't working for us" by overcoming this tidal excuse. "Is the tide ever going to change?!?"

"It's So Hot the Fish are Asking for a Swim."

On the lake, the dog days of summer can suck.

It's hot as blue blazes. Not a breath of wind. It's late July and the humidity seems to be so thick you could cut it with a knife. Fish tend to move slower. They find deeper holes and shade under docks or vegetation. They are lethargic just like the lumbering buffoons above the surface of the water. We have ways to provide relief in the form of conditioned air (AC), cold drinks, shade on demand, cool showers, and a plunge into a spring-fed lake. The fish are stuck and that can suck for fishing. The bite is slower due to bait not moving about, and our larger targeted fish are more comfortable simply doing nothing, eating less, and working only when required—sounds like us! So, anglers tend to catch less during the dog days of summer.

While our ice chests become heavier with more hydration drinks and dehydration drinks (beer), we do not normally have a problem with space in the cooler for fish. Many times, we cut the day shorter to get back home or throw in the tube, skis, or kneeboard. Sandbar or "yacht club" activities pick up during these days and that is likely not a coincidence. Back-to-School flyers are coming in the mail and the days are getting shorter. All are monumental excuses for fewer fishing trips and less luck on the water this time of year. Don't let the dog days suck the life out of you—your rods and reels will get back in the swing with the "fall pattern" that is just a few weeks ahead. "As hot as it is out here, I can't blame these fish for not biting!"

Did you Know?

United States anglers spend over seven billion dollars a year on fishing gear. We take this moment to thank you for your contributions. People think you are rich. No, you have more invested in your fishing gear than your retirement plan.

"FLASH . . . ONE MISSISSIPPI, TWO MISSISSIPPI, THREE MISSISSIBOOOOOM . . . LET'S GO!"

Lightning and fishing don't mix. In fact, lightning deaths are not limited to the golf course, as one might think. Lightning deaths while fishing occur two-thirds more often than golfing, and lightning while boating deaths are more than twice as common than golf. A common reason for cutting a summertime fishing trip short is fear of being struck by lightning and calling it a day. Many of us become highly trained meteorologists and voluntarily take on the role of "counter." We observe the lightning strike and count (as fast as we can) the number of seconds until we hear thunder so we can, with confidence, predict the direction and distance from the bolt.

As a temptation, oftentimes before a storm, fish can become aggressive feeders, begging for us to make a few more casts. We ask you, our fellow anglers, can we make a pact to get off the water or bank when we know what is coming and avoid our potential demise? Of course, this can work to your advantage. The next time you come home empty handed, you have at an excuse at the ready: "We would have caught a boatload if not for that crazy lightning!"

"Too Still (No Current or Wind)."

Blow, wind, blow!

It is hard to imagine, considering how many trips have been scratched or should have been scratched due to howling wind, that *anyone* would ever say it is too *still* to catch fish. We've heard it and seen it ourselves. We've been on the Gulf when it is so calm that the horizon disappears. There is not a ripple on the water and a fly or floating grass can be seen on the surface seemingly frozen. The smallest of lures sounds like a grenade hitting the water while floating line dances about as the retrieve begins alerting anything within one hundred yards that there is nothing natural about this situation.

"We just need a little movement," or "Fish really seem to bite the rougher it is out here" statements start to slip out, knowing we pray for days like this. So why is this excuse accepted . . . or is it? One thought is that without the distraction of a ripple lapping the side of the boat or a breath of whistling wind, a heightened awareness causes an angler to second guess his bait and presentation. With this heightened awareness comes second guessing of bait and presentation. Increased backlashes or knots. Bad casts and poor boat maneuverability. All things which *should* increase bites, but because of our distraction of calm it does the opposite. "Just a little breeze would be nice to turn these fish on."

"I FORGOT TO SPIT ON MY BAIT."

From sitting in your lucky chair during the big game, to wearing your lucky socks for an important meeting, humans are notorious for looking for a not-so-scientific edge. And, as you may have guessed, fishing is no different. Another common superstition is that if you spit on your bait, it can help bring you some luck. But if you happen to forget, don't worry. The next time you strike out like Reggie Jackson on the baseball diamond (Jackson has more whiffs than anyone in baseball history) just explain it with, "I don't know what I was thinking, but I completely forgot to spit on my bait."

Did You Know?

The most expensive lure ever made is encrusted with diamonds and gold, and costs $1 million dollars. Can you imagine the feeling of setting the hook and breaking off this lure into a giant log in muddy water ten feet under the surface?

"HUNGOVER—CAUGHT A BUZZ BUT SHOULD BE CATCHING FISH."

Getting green behind the gills! Not from the seas or the motion of the ocean, but from the last call that sounded like a great idea at the local watering hole at 1:00 a.m. We launch the boat in *five hours*! The excitement of the end of a long week before a fishing trip, which has been in the works since who-knows-when, can lead to a heavy pour. Sometimes the wake-up call comes, and the buzz hasn't quite worn off yet, so up and at 'em it is. Stumble through the morning routine and catch a ride with your partner to the boat.

And then it hits you. You couldn't down the honey bun from the gas station and quite frankly the headache splintering your forehead is only distracted by the need to hurl! This is not what you or your crew had in mind for chumming. And your prospects of fishing and catching are simply floating away in the form of a slick behind the boat. Can you hurl and rally? Can you get some Vienna sausages and a coke down? Do you partake in a little "hair of the dog" and pop open an ice-cold beer as the sun is coming up? For as long as there have been boats, booze, and fishing, there have been green-behind-the-gills anglers nursing a hangover. Catch a buzz at the bar, but don't forget to leave a little throttle for the big one.

"TOO HUNGRY."

Fishing requires focus. Focus requires food. Have you ever noticed, especially with kids, once you get on the water, your stomach magically expands to a vast bottomless pit and there is a direct connection between your mouth and your massive empty stomach?! You see, being on a boat requires one to constantly use muscles to provide balance from the "motion of the ocean." Your sea-legs are working, along with your core, to keep you balanced while your casting, reeling, and motion of your retrieve is constant work, which you are not accustomed to while sitting at the office or on the couch. Without a plan for a snack, your chances for success are negatively impacted. This plan should, at a minimum, include your favorite pack of crackers, beef jerky, or chips. The real MVPs take it a step further and bring chicken wings, a pre-made bologna sandwich, or even leftovers. This is how it's done. It also allows for a mental break to enjoy a quality refueling and contemplation about your next move, whether it be location, bait, presentation, or a combination thereof.

Feed yourself, then feed the fish—don't get hangry on the water.

"TOO MANY WHINERS ON BOARD!"

Fishing is a sport akin to baseball, football, and even golf—where the power of momentum and confidence produces great results. Believing in every cast and every twitch, that at any second the big one could bite and bring a power struggle, releases endorphins and emotions as addictive and unique as a win in a major sport.

In the same vein . . . a whiner is a major problem. When you have one along for your trip, they can gripe aloud with complaints of the conditions, the lack of action, or even what they would rather be doing. A whiner can be contagious and bring the trip possibilities down quickly.

A helpful antivenom to this poison needs to be quickly applied. Nip it in the bud. Take the high road and ask for them to help get a fish in the box and tell a story of how a similar trip yielded a lifelong memory. Or, simply let them know they can swim back or shut it. At this point, the whiner on board is given an opportunity within their control to be a team player or pout it out until they get off your boat for the last time. "Thanks for joining us—we had a blast, but your whining was a drag!"

"No Beer Onboard."

Beer attracts all kinds of fish and not having any on board is a brazen and unnecessary detractor from catching fish. A curse! Many anglers for some reason think it is ok to drink a beer while fishing at hours during which they would not dream of doing so in any other setting. It shall bring them luck and lead to a more relaxed and favorable presentation to the fish, as they pause for another swig. So, when the crew opens the cooler to grab a "sausage biscuit" (a.k.a., a beer before sunrise), or to help change their luck when nothing is biting, and they find an ice chest which is flush with water bottles and soda . . . get ready for the excuses.

How can one expect to catch a single fish without catching a buzz?! The attention to which lures to use, which shoreline to attack, the retrieve speed of lures, and all normal fishing tactics goes by the wayside. Excuses start to sneak their way into the conversation and before you know it, your trip is cut short. So, is it the fishing that we are after or the beer buzz?

"Let's go get some beer—we need to change our luck."

"SEASICKNESS: THE ORIGINAL AND LEAST EFFECTIVE CHUMMING TECHNIQUE."

If you've ever been seasick, there is only one panacea: to place your two feet on dry land. The first indication is the thought "Am I feeling queasy?" and from there it is *over*. Gone like a falling tide on a full moon. Next up, the sweaty brow and the rumble of the stomach. The thought of what was for breakfast and dinner the night before . . . damn, you know this is about to be chum.

Everyone else on board is in heaven. Catching fish after fish, making for a great trip offshore. Hell, it took you an hour to get out here and you lost sight of land ten miles out. And here you are about to ruin it. Not only is an upset stomach an ineffective and poor attempt for chumming, it is a guarantee for no fish for the victim(s) and almost always results in an inexcusable excuse to return to the dock.

Pro Tip: Know yourself and buy one of many over-the-counter or prescription treatments for motion sickness. We don't need a human chum-producer on board—we bought chum at the tackle shop.

"I SLEPT IN."

Early bird gets the bream! It's common to launch your boat before sunrise to navigate safely in twilight to your favorite spot. There is something about casting to a picturesque sunrise and catching fish, while everyone else is asleep in their warm and comfortable bed.

Pushing the snooze button or forgetting to set an alarm is one thing, but even more despicable of an excuse is making the conscious decision to roll over and skip the trip. Sleeping in is one of those feels-so-good joys of life, but 100 percent of the time is a bad decision in fishing. By the time 9:00 a.m. rolls around, you are kicking yourself for not getting your lazy ass out of bed. Your excuse to loaf around is eating at you and you commit to never let it happen again and you even ponder . . . *can I go* now? Heck no. It is hot, the wind is up, and the real anglers are already reeling the fish two at a time in your spot.

You snooze you lose in fishing—don't be a lazy ass and go catch a bass.

"MY EXPECTATIONS WERE TOO LOW."

There is a fine line between being overconfident and expecting to catch nothing. Setting low expectations can become reality if anglers do not overcome the challenges of the bite. Is it due to the actual conditions of the lake or is it because of the lack of desire driven by the low expectations set by the anglers?

With seasonality, water temperatures, moon phases, and weather, there are true factors, which we all should factor into our enthusiasm and likelihood of success. But anyone who has fished long enough has been very surprised by a trip where the bite was strong, and you never missed a fish. These trips boost our confidence and expectations for future trips. The flip side is a skunk job where we wonder why we would every fish again and if we should take up golfing. With experience, we should find a balance of a "good day" of a daily bag complete with mid-sized fish on a steady bite.

With newcomers or out-of-towners on board, we all should have reasonably low expectations in mind, but every cast and approach should come with the same level of excitement and intent to succeed. Low expectations are excusable but can't be leaned upon year-round as your go-to excuse.

"We probably won't catch anything today, but we need to run the boat anyway."

"The Cricket Cage Fell Overboard."

To an angler, the small cylinder metal screen cage with a red plastic top and bottom can be recognized in an instant as a marvelous invention, which allows our big paws to enter and the tiny insects to not escape. The engineering and calculation of this contraption is nothing short of amazing.

In another stunning display of our masterful intelligence, we humans have learned to cut a potato in half or quarters or smaller to "feed" the crickets for a night or two in between trips. We carry the cricket cage with tender care, as if it were full of diamonds of the rough. How then have we, the geniuses, allowed the cage to fall into the water? Without swift, life-saving acts, our bait becomes a mash of sharp legs and mushy material which resembles soaking wet wheat bread. A dead cricket is useless and messy, and the extraction is less enjoyable in clumps and without a bare hook on the other hand anxiously awaiting impalement. Hasn't happened to you yet? Lucky you!

Did You Know?

Sharks are actually the only fish that have eyelids, which are useful for protecting the eyes when attacking prey.

"THE FISH ARE ON FIRE—LET'S GO BACK OUT ON THE WATER TOMORROW."

You have two days to fish this weekend, and everything is lining up. The weather, the moon, and the reports have been stellar. You hit the lake and from the first cast until you decide to "leave them biting," it was EPIC. This is a day to remember.

Head held high, you hope the boat ramp is busier than usual so you have an audience to tout your successes. Your phone is filled with selfies, ruler shots, and a livewell full of fish marking your best day yet. On the way home, you call a coworker who is a wishful angler who always thinks you catch more than professionals on TV.

"You want to go tomorrow morning? I'm *dialed in*. Like fishing in a barrel."

Everything lines up the same as the previous day and your excitement . . . well, it dwindles with every cast and no bite. Fishing the same baits, the same shore, the same presentation, and nothing. Not even a nibble. Your friend makes a comment about swinging by the fish market on their way home to put filets in their empty cooler.

Your fishing experience is not a lock—even on the same lake, shore, or dock, just a night's sleep in between. What can you do but lament: "The fish were on fire yesterday, but alas, no such luck today."

"I RAN OUT OF GAS."

"I thought we had half a tank!" Gas gauges are notoriously faulty on boats of age—those that are "seasoned" well. Gauges also read very differently, depending on how a boat sits on a trailer as compared to sitting on the water. Understanding your gas gauge is important as you get to know your boat. Also, knowing your GPH (gallons per hour) is important to do the math as you map out your range for any given fishing adventure.

There is nothing more disappointing, and unsafe, than running out of fuel on a boat. Your lifeline to the shore has been eliminated. The greatest catches ever are nullified when one has either forgotten to refuel, burned too much fuel in pursuit of the big one, or otherwise neglected to carry the fundamental responsibility of ensuring enough fuel is on board for the trip.

As a fishing companion, this question is one which should always be answered (along with another question which involves a four-letter word that starts with "p" and ends with "g"): "Do we have enough fuel?"

The response, "I think we have a half a tank" is a whole reason to check and top her off.

"I HAD TO TOW SOMEONE IN."

"Y'all need a tow?" could very well be the kindest words you could shout across the bow to a boater in need.

It also could be the best way to ensure your fishing trip turns into a charity event. If you have fished long enough, you have seen (or been on board) a boat with the cowling off the motor, Mom on the bow with her arms crossed, kids frustrated, hungry, and hot. And Dad fidgets with everything he can think of to get the tower of power running.

Boats over sixteen feet in many states are required to have a paddle. Did you ever think a paddle could be made so small to fit in the tiny compartment under the console of a boat? It was "perfect" at the time of purchase to check the old box of boating safety. This perfect paddle could be rivaled by a wooden spoon in grammy's kitchen. No way in hell it is moving an eighteen-foot bowrider with a smoking motor on a smoking hot Fourth of July!

Be sure next time you see a boat in distress and a crew in disbelief to idle over and make their day with the love language of broken down bowriders . . .

"Too Lazy."

"I think I'll go next week, I'm too tired."

Looking at the top excuses for any activity, from work to pleasure, this one has to be a top contender. Anything worth doing requires effort, planning, physical exertion, and oftentimes hours of standing or otherwise flailing about in an attempt to catch a fish.

Laying around the house is easier, right? The regret sinks in hard about .005 seconds after it is too late to carry out your plans as the honey-dos begin to enter into your head organically or directly from your "honey." Time flies from the couch as episodes turn from a few to a binge session. Next thing you know, your rumbling stomach tells you it's time to eat lunch and an afternoon nap plan is underway.

The shame of it all? You have done absolutely nothing and the experience of a day on the water is lost. Next weekend? Don't let "I think I'll go next week, I'm too tired" ruin it two weeks in a row.

"TOO MANY HYPER ANGLERS!"

Simmer down and we might get a bite!

Fishing with kids is as important to the sport as it is memorable for the young angler. Patience is a critical virtue when it comes to being trapped in a small space or perched upon the bank with a jumping bean full of enormous energy, lots of questions, and the ability to make a mess in the blink of an eye. Fishing is tricky when it comes to hyper kids or adults who just can't keep still. Whether it is jumping up and down, moving about, constantly asking questions, or hooking, tangling, and knotting everything in sight, a hyper angler can be difficult to handle.

The trick to fishing is the exertion of energy largely occurs *after* the hook has been set. Hence the problem. One must focus, present a bait, be relatively quiet (in most cases), and be ready to engage. Only then does the use of muscles throughout the body and mind begin. Finding the best solution to channeling hyper crew members may be found with a bag of snacks, music, telling fish tales, and even providing the rookie angler with a "safe rod" with a barbless or hookless rig which can be cast with low risk of disaster. Either way, maintaining your sanity will lead to more enjoyment for all.

"Simmer down young'n and we might get a bite!"

"I Hate the Full Moon Bite—the Fish Feed All Night!"

A full moon occurs every 29.5 days, after making its way through a full lunar phase cycle. This bright, big-ole moon that we all stare up at in awe has caused many fishing trips to be a flop. Funny thing is, the moon is only truly "full" for one night, but the impacts of the moon's brightness can last much longer. To the average angler looking up at the dern thing, it may appear to be full for as many as three days. Many anglers avoid the full moon altogether because of personal experience or tales from others belly-aching about it.

The most legitimate reason for lackluster full moon action on the water is because the bright light exposes bait and gives predator fish prime feeding opportunities far beyond the regular daylight hours. In short, they feed more, so the bite intensity is significantly dulled to smithereens. It's only at twilight of sunrise and sunset that the bait is at its best on a full moon. Any angler who tells you they like to fish on the full moon is either an optimist at heart, has a location which outperforms most, or they just want to spend time with you on the water. Go ahead and join them, but when you return without a haul, remind them: "I hate the full moon bite—the fish feed all night!"

"NO MOON—WE FISHED WHEN THE FISH RESTED—NOT DURING THE MAJOR FEEDING PERIOD."

The "dark moon," or the last visible crescent of the waning moon, is the darkest of the 29.5 lunar phase cycle. Like the full moon, this phase of the cycle lasts between 1.5 and 3.5 days, causing fantastic sleep, the darkest nights, and arguably the biggest bites for most anglers. But why do some anglers balk at this frenzied spell? This can be most likely explained, unfortunately: They missed the major or minor feeding periods, which are intense during this moon phase. To be blunt, the fish just smashed it for an hour and a half, and they needed a break.

Every day, a major and minor feeding period is documented and should be monitored closely so you can prepare for the feast. For many unlucky anglers, they are "lines in" a half hour after the big buffet shuts down. Just like your local trough after a fifth plate of your heart's desire, you want to walk it off or take a nap. New moon fish, when caught between feeding periods, are seen with other fish in their throats, vomiting them on the deck, or pooping as their bodies bulge from the binge. And, just like that, it is time to go— before the scaled behemoths are ready for another round. "Let's go fish the hour exactly between the major feeding periods" is the mantra of a skinny angler.

"Would You Like to Book a Charter on the Honeymoon? On Second Thought . . ."

Honeymoons often find newlyweds in some of the most beautiful locales across the globe. From the Bahamas to Hawaii to the Florida Keys, these beautiful places are filled with boats, captains, and, most importantly, fish looking to jump into the boat. Then there is the "schedule of events," which is presumably preconceived by the couple: wineries, shopping, sightseeing, dining; not a fish in sight, except maybe on your plate. So it goes.

Relaxing under a cabana, with a tropical drink in hand, looking out onto the deep blue ocean, your wandering eye spots a boat rigged for mahi, wahoo, marlin, tuna. Your mind begins to turn over the possibilities. Unless your relationship was founded upon the beauty and benefits of fishing, or you have the rare partnership approach to fishing, then this one is not a likely desired outcome, as a disagreement will likely ensue.

Thinking of getting married? Engaged? Start planting the seeds now and book a charter for your honeymoon. Thank us later.

"... Snap out of it, you dummy! You're on your honeymoon!"

"O-Dark-Thirty came O-Too-Early!"

Fishing at the crack of dawn comes with incredible serenity. "Watching the outdoors wake up" is a common feeling many anglers proudly share upon reflection of the first birds singing, the glow of an early sunrise, and even the headlights glow at the boat ramp.

But starting early comes with its risks, too. When the sunrise is a documented time, and you know exactly how long it takes to rise, grab your coffee, dress, drive to the ramp, and launch, why on earth do you get up *hours* earlier?! In doing so, you may have spent hours of peak focus and drive by waiting impatiently for the ball of fire to rise in the East. This wasted time could be used resting your weary head and dreaming about hooking the lunker.

Take your beauty rest, Captain E. Riser, and spend those extra hours in bed. At day's end, you will be raring and ready to go and your motivation to stay out on the boat will be extended. Don't let O-Dark-Thirty come too early, if you want to catch more fish!

"I STARTED TOO LATE."

This episode of *We Got Skunked* was brought to you by "The Crack of Noon Fishing Crew."

Many of us fall into the "early bird" or "night owl" categories and use that excuse for everything under the sun. If there is any excuse in this book that is inexcusable, this one has to be it. Starting too late and subsequently not catching fish is a no-brainer. It's a valid excuse for not catching fish, but one that cannot be accepted by your fellow anglers.

Let's stand strong, together, and ensure we have our alarm clocks set, our schedules cleared, and our minds aligned so that we *will not* start the coveted day on the water late. Treat this day as your wedding day, and don't be late. Don't be a member of "The Crack of Noon Fishing Crew."

Did You Know?

The most popular game fish in the United States is the largemouth bass. More than 30 million bass-fishing anglers support a $60 billion industry. One in every five Americans set the hook in a bass each year.

"Pass the Aloe and Advil . . . I'm Burnt to a 'Fare Thee Well!'"

The sunburn excuse Rule Number 1: This excuse is only valid the second day of fishing on a multiple-trip excursion.

Day One: The excitement and weather were level ten. You remember the beer, the bait, the rods and reels, and have a game plan crafted that is unbeatable. Pass the sunscreen. Forgot it. Cut-off sleeves and ball cap. Sunglasses are at the house. Shorts and flip-flops and pale-ass feet. This is a red lobster in the making.

Day Two: The pain is sickening. The pores have been sizzled to a deep purple-red with certain blisters beginning to crust over. Tops of feet shine and with each step wrinkle into a jellyfish sting. The hands, nose, ears, and neck are hot to the touch. Fishing is the last thing on his mind and while he may join for tomorrow's fishing trip, he shall gladly take on the role of DJ, bartender, and Captain Complainer! Rule Number 2: Fair-skinned anglers, you know who you are. Lather up the first day and get your fish on!

If you do misplace your SPF 100 and manage to walk away with your hands fried and empty, simply say, "If I hadn't forgotten my darn sunscreen, I would surely have caught a big one."

"I Don't Have a License—Now I Have a Fine to Pay."

"May I see your license?" is a question to which game wardens across the country should never hear any response other than, "Sure, I have it right here." Technology in fishing licenses has evolved over the years, with state-of-the-art mobile applications and online licensing systems that provide tasteful reminders throughout the year that your licenses are expiring.

Many states have auto-renew options to ensure you are never out of compliance. While mobile apps store licenses, the old paper copy will do, and even a collector card with cool artwork can fit in your wallet. Whichever state you fish in, you are covered with options to buy a license quickly, securely, and easily for yourself and your crew. If you have a bait mate that says they can't fish with you because they don't have a license, then help them out by buying them a short-term license, or splurge and buy an annual license if you like them. Each license purchase sends funds directly into conservation and management of the sport we all love—be ready and proudly display your license when a warden rightly asks you, "May I see your license?" If you can't produce it, get ready to pay the fine for doing the crime.

"I Kept an Undersized Fish."

"Peench its tail . . . it'll ride" are famous last words for an unethical angler who knowingly harvests undersized fish. Pinching the tail to measure the minnow of the deep to try to reach the slot size is an acceptable practice in most states. Keeping a fish that is regulated and documented to be a certain size to stink the grease is not acceptable.

Interestingly, the majority of cases of anglers unlawfully keeping undersized fish are often accompanied by over-the-bag limit and no (or expired) licenses. This is company that no one wants to keep. Game wardens can sniff out a suspect from a mile away and the undersized fish in the box is the easiest way to turn a pitiful trip into a costly one. Don't do it, encourage it, or make this a part of your angling experience! It might get you a ride to the big house!

Did You Know?

In 1959, an Australian fisherman named Alfred Dean caught the biggest fish on record . . . a great white shark that weighed 2,664 pounds. "Deep Blue" is a tagged female Great White, which is at least 20 feet long and over 5,500 pounds. If anyone would like to crush Dean's record . . . we're going to need a bigger boat.

"I Released an Oversized Fish."

The thrill of an over-slot trophy catch can only be fully realized by the final step in the memorable process—the release. A trophy fish has earned this right, having survived countless predators, miserable cold, dreadful heat, floods, drought, and by no surprise to most of us, repeated attempts of countless anglers trying to catch it with their lure of choice. A trophy fish is a breeder that keeps our stocks full. Yes, this fine specimen swam upriver for miles, dove to depths without light, navigated locks and dams, nearly perished due to lack of water, oxygen, or food. Take in all its glory, admire its resilience, and toss it back. If it's the reason you come back to the dock without a lip to grip, share your new memory with pride that you caught and released a breeder, and pay attention to how it makes you feel. It's addicting. Join us in shouting from the boat, "Over-slot fish belong in the bay!"

"We Left the Rods at the Dock."

"You said you were getting the rods?!" We're easing up to the honey hole. We have made the long, fast, and exhausting run across the lake, a run that takes up a third of our available fishing time. The anticipation of the lunker bass crushing our top-water frog as it slithers quietly through the lily pads is *real*! We unbuckle our PFDs and an eerie quiet overcomes us. Captain, chest out a bit, rotates his shoulders back and forth in a rolling motion while a look of both cocky and smooooooth comes across his face as he quietly lowers the trolling motor into the water. A split second before turning to grab his perfectly rigged bait-caster, it hits him: he doesn't even turn around.

A deep gaze into the trees in the distance. An adjustment of the neck and a tip of the cap. Without saying a word, he turns to his first mate, as if he can produce what the captain had come to realize, only after a painful sigh of "NO!"—an expression with the tone of pain similar to setting the hook into your mid-thigh level with rusty treble hooks. We all know now: The rods are in the truck. All locked up in the back under the cover. Nothing left to do other than sit back and buckle back up the PFDs, start a belly laugh, and state the obvious.

"I'M BROKE!"

Technically, to go fishing all you need is a stick, a rope, a hook, and a worm. But if you want to really make any headway, you're going to need to invest a few Benjamins. Between the rods, clothes, bait—and don't even get us started on the boat—it can all add up quickly. But what happens if you're just an average Joe with a low-paying job, a few kids, and a mortgage or rent that eats up your paycheck?

It goes without saying that there might not be a lot left over to spend on your favorite hobby. But why not use this to your advantage? The next time you strike out on the water, just go home, and tell your family and friends, "If I had the money, I would have caught a barrel full of fish. Unfortunately . . . I'm broke!"

Did You Know?

In 2009, Illinois was the first state to incorporate bass fishing as a high school sport.

"FORGOT MY LUNCH."

"I could eat my arm off right now. We have to head in to eat."

The state of "hangry" is well documented. It can set in quickly and fiery amongst company or activities that aren't as tolerable as fishing. You see, fishing has the ability to quickly become a fast, as the result of poor planning. Forgetting to pack a lunch is an inconvenient truth which will eventually catch up to anglers. Oddly enough, when "the bite" is on with fishing, the symptoms of attitudinal shifts, growling stomachs, and lack of focus are kept at bay for extended times beyond the explanation of dieticians and scientists alike.

However, let the bite slow down or stop, and the hangry symptoms do begin, rather quickly, to enter the dialog.

"What do you think about heading in to grab a bite?" might be the first indication that the rumble of the tumble may be ending the trip sooner than anticipated. After a short string of three casts with no bites, backlash due to the loss of focus, or an untimely, minor wind gust, one may find themselves pulling the plug.

"KIDS."

Travel ball, cheer, volleyball, dance recitals, the flu, final exams, pick up/drop offs for sleepovers—the excuses kids introduce are long in number and long in years. We have friends who have been damn-near professional anglers with time, equipment, and expertise to fish with the best of the best, who might as well have been thrown in jail for a ten-year sentence (or longer) of no fishing. Some still wear fishing apparel, sunglasses, and hats to pretend they still go. Some of the smart ones "winterize" their boats, gear, and tackle and place them in storage for easy access during the two to three weeks between seasons.

Trouble is, these breaks occur at intervals on the calendar for other reasons such as holidays or end-of-school sessions, which are inevitably clogged with other activities. The real smart ones? They somehow have the ability to come to terms with reality and pull the hardest trigger of all: They sell out. They sell all their gear and even boats. By the time their sentence is over they'll be sitting on outdated equipment which will be out of service and somewhat technologically obsolete, giving them a disadvantage, so they cash in and use those funds for well-timed guided trips with top-notch guides in peak seasons. They save up for when they have "served their time" and can reload with the best and newest gear. One day, weekend activities and parental responsibilities start to dwindle, the kids grow up, and a new chapter in their fishing story begins.

"Forgot the Bait."

Some trips are close and convenient to the "hill." The trips are close to the house, the boat ramp is convenient with plenty of parking, and the fishing grounds are so close your motor doesn't even warm up fully. These are the locations where the fish aren't picky eaters, all anglers are more relaxed, and the trip doesn't require a second mortgage for fuel.

Other trips are miles upon miles of open water or winding rivers to navigate and "half the battle is just getting there." This is prime territory for forgetting something as a minor inconvenience. You know, a pair of pliers, or a towel. Maybe even sunscreen. But if you forget the bait, you are up shit's little creek without a paddle, per se. Whether the bait is fresh or frozen, if it is not on board when you get to hell's half acre to fish, you are done.

When you figure it out, all you can do is laugh and proudly tout, "We got beer, bologna sandwiches, and no bait."

"THE GREATEST TWO DAYS OF A BOATER'S LIFE: THE DAY THEY BUY A BOAT AND THE DAY THEY SELL A BOAT."

Boats are vessels of freedom. They provide the endless joy of the open water and freedom from the stresses of the daily grind—feelings of floating and flying mixed with a touch of pure joy by your family and friends aboard, and the challenge and reward of a day of catching lots of fish. Cleaning a fish-slimed boat, whether new or antique, never has the dissatisfaction of cleaning a car, a house, or even dishes.

When buying a boat, the excitement produces a high only matched when pushing off the dock for the first time with rods, reels, and tackle ready to see what one can do in their new fishing machine. With each new boat purchase, a dreaded day lies ahead: The day she is sold to the next angler ... but is it sweet or bitter? A relief or a deep dark depression? Either way you have lost your direct access to fish. This is a fishing disadvantage unlike any other. Do you beg your neighbor or family? Do you rent? Do you wade or pier fish? With every glimmer of hope for alternatives to having your own vessel of freedom brings the reality of the darkest days of a boater's and angler's life ... NO BOAT!

Feeling fishy ... call your friend and offer to buy the gas, beer, and bring the bananas! Because clearly you would have reeled in a ton if you simply had a boat.

"I HAVE TO TAKE CARE OF MY PARENTS."

Father time catches us all.

The earliest memories for many of us are spending time as a young angler with Mom and Dad. They took the time, at an early age, to teach us. They had the patience and desire to untangle messes, answer question upon question, rise before the sun, and drive long distances into the night for us. We became better anglers with their help. As we grew, we started to even out in skill. Then we began to fish more with friends, and perhaps our own children. Just as our parents' patience was tested, ours is as well, but we continue on with the same pride to pass on a tradition like no other.

As the years begin to pass quicker, our parents begin to slow down, and we have to be around more often. This slowdown allows us the opportunity to care for them, and in doing so we may miss out on or cut short some fishing trips. Not only is this excuse valid and necessary, but it also allows for some valuable time to recount some of the best trips. Remember the embarrassing time we nearly burned the truck down at the boat ramp because Dad's bifocal reading glasses were placed perfectly on the dash for hours while we fished, at an angle which magnified the sunlight to burn a large smokey hole through the entire dash? Repeating that story for years, much to our delight, is special. If we had returned to find our truck in a pile of ash, we would've certainly blamed it on the "rough locals" in the area from whom we had received scowls earlier due to our out-of-state plates. Recalling these memories through conversations with aging parents can be as rewarding and important as making new ones. Father time catches us all. Even the ones who got us hooked.

Did You Know?

The first fishing lures were made from stone, bone, or wood. Primitive lure-making and fishing is making a comeback for many who feel the need to challenge themselves more than us!

"I Took Up Golf."

Tired of not catching fish and sinking our 401ks into every "advantage" available in the local sporting goods store, we made the decision to take up . . . golf. Are we idiots or just desperate for time away from our brutal realities? We suck at fishing. We can't suck this bad at golf, right? Excuses abound for double bogey's, shanks, and whiffs. Why not swap out breakoffs, backlashes, and gaff misses for a landlubber's dream—golf.

Now, the ultimate excuse for not catching fish? A tee time.

Funny thing is, unlike fishing, a bad day of golf doesn't always beat a good day in the office. It can be a frustrating sport and a dose of reality that lands squarely on the responsibility of the golfer. An errant drive, a duff on an open fairway shot, or a four-foot putt left a foot short. The frustration can boil over to a sailor's choice of cursing and name-calling one cannot repeat.

The myriad of excuses for not catching any fish while tying off the boat to the dock brings with it a balance of adventure and humility while our newfound excuse of playing golf is perhaps the lamest in this book. Hit the lakes, not the links, friends.

"TOO MANY PASSENGERS ONBOARD."

"ALL ABOARD! Are you sure we have room?"

Boats have US Coast Guard Maximum Capacity plates which set the maximum persons (*or* pounds) and maximum recommended horsepower. These recommendations are for safety purposes and should be taken seriously and can be used either in support of a crowd or as a deterrent.

What is not likely considered by the Coast Guard in establishing these recommendations is the flailing about with six-foot rods in every direction and razor-sharp barbed hooks at the end of the line. One can certainly plan a miserable day on the water by maxing out the persons on board with an expectation that each person will simultaneously fish or engage in fishing. Tangled lines which closely resemble the perfect home for a pair of nesting wrens are a given. Damaged gear in the form of broken rods and lost tackle are highly likely. Hooks to the back, neck, leg, or arms are increasingly more prone to happen, as opposed to fish pulling on the end of a line. The art of the captain's ability to set their own capacities is the real catch.

When the "all aboard" conversation starts to take off—be sure to have your elevator pitch ready in the name of the US Coast Guard Maximum Capacity, which you can enforce. "This is a fishing boat . . . not a ferry service!"

"MOVED."

WANTED: JOB TRANSFER TO BASS CAPITAL OF THE WORLD.

Some of the most stressful and carefully considered decisions anyone has to make will revolve around relocation to a new city or state. New friends, jobs, homes, and all the fun that surrounds touching everything you own and packing it into a moving truck only to unpack it all again in a new house or apartment. Before all other qualifications, we must screen our real estate agents first by their fishing knowledge and their willingness to take us on a comprehensive a lake-by-lake tour ranking in order of quality of the fishery, boat ramps, and sandbar weekend shenanigans of our new town.

Any relocation brings with it new waters. New boat ramps and seasons. New species targets and regulations. Rarely are there not decent fishing opportunities in virtually any corner of the globe, but some are richer compared to others.

Social media, message boards, and local lore give all of us access to the same information on where to fish and for what. The sooner we pinpoint this key information after a move, the sooner we will find our new digs acceptable and downright enjoyable.

"I Got Tired trying to Reel in a Shark for Two Hours."

Fishing can bring out the best in people. From a friendly "hello" on the water to a helpful tow for a stalled boat. Not only does fishing lead to good deeds, it can also end up providing us with a will that we never knew we had. If you've ever been deep-sea fishing and have engaged in a massive struggle to reel in a mammoth fish, you know what we're talking about. However, even with the greatest of efforts, every fisherman knows that it's not always a Hollywood ending. So, the next time the angry sea leaves you feeling a bit of anger yourself, just explain your failure with, "I was exhausted after battling a shark for the last two hours that barely escaped."

Did You Know?

The world's largest fish is the whale shark, which can grow up to forty feet in length and weigh up to twenty tons.

"I HAD TO GO BACK TO WORK."

Ahhh, to be retired with money in your pocket and the ability to go fishing whenever, and wherever, you'd like. Dare to dream! In the meantime, if you're like us, you need to find the time to squeeze in a couple of hours on the water when you can get the chance. And like most weekend warriors, that normally revolves around work. But what happens if your boss is riding you to work extra hours? Or you have your own business, and it requires around-the-clock attention? There are going to be times when duty calls and you simply can't spend as much time as you'd like trying to reel in a couple of big ones. Not to worry. You can use this to your advantage. The next time you come home without the big trophy, just say, "If I just had a little more time, and didn't have to get back to work, I definitely would have reeled in a winner."

"I Had to Spend Time with My Family."

Fishing and family go together like peanut butter and jelly, summertime and a cold beer, The Fourth of July and apple pie. They're simply a perfect combination. Fishing with our parents and kids has given us some of the most special memories. But what happens, dare we even think it, when one or more of your family members has an aversion to the great outdoors? What happens when a piano recital or class trip requires your presence? Of course your kids and parents come first, so feel free to tell anyone that has a close-knit family, "I'm lucky to be surrounded by so much love, but if I had a clan that loved fishing more, I would have caught a boat load."

"Fish Are On the Bed."

"She won't bite, but she might move the bait."

Giant bedding bass present a fascinating opportunity to catch a trophy fish. In clear, shallow water, the near-perfect circle-shaped bed she has fanned out to spawn upon is in some ways is both a target and an amazing circle of life. She will carefully find the perfect depth, cover, and soil type to begin readying her bed. Over several days of hard work and prep, she both grows in girth and in the size of the bed leading up to her spawn. In a motherly act of protection, she will defend her bed fiercely, scaring and carefully dragging off predatorial crayfish or even small turtles.

This presents the opportunity to pitch a plastic worm or lizard and hookset a wall-hanging bass with a bulging belly. It also is an opportunity to let 'em be. If you can think about the long-view and consider letting her defend her bed from natural non-human predators, then you may be paid dividends in the future with many more bass days ahead. If it is legal in your area and you want to set that hook and land her, then go for it, but remember: she isn't biting your bait . . . she's just moving it.

"THE COWS WERE LAYING DOWN."

"Fish aren't bitin'."

"Why do you say that?"

"Cows are laying down."

Many days, we pass the pasture and the cattle farm to notice the cows are all laying down. They find the shade under the canopy of a big oak, and chew on cud along with an occasional tail whip at biting flies. This is the most trusted and long-standing indicator of a non-feeding period. Check it yourself. Pull up your favorite major feeding period app and next time you will see the cows sprawled about the farm, none of them standing or grazing on the grass.

If you see them marching at a quick clip and mowing down the grass to the nubs and almost in a determined pace to nowhere . . . find yourself a rod and head to the farm pond. The fish are biting. So, the next time you are with an old-timer ask them if they have known this old wives' tale to be true. Better yet, when you see the cows lying down, throw it out there and see if they bite on it. Let's all help pass this on by telling the young anglers about this tale.

"I JUST NEED TO WIN THE LOTTERY."

So, you have your gear, your best bait, a cooler full of your favorite beverages, and, of course, the old boat is all gassed up. It's the perfect formula for a fun-filled day on the water. But as we all know, times can get tough. The economy can turn on a dime. And unfortunately, that can lead to cutbacks and layoffs. If the unthinkable happens, and you find yourself with bills to pay, a family to feed, and an empty bank account, you may need to make some tough decisions. If you are out pounding the pavement, looking for work, and don't have the time or money to engage in the most worthwhile of endeavors, just tell your friends, "I'd love to go fishing this weekend, but times are tough, and I had to sell the old boat. Once I win the lottery, I'll have plenty of time to catch a ton of fish."

"My Boat is *Still* in the Shop."

B.O.A.T. ("Break out another thousand") is inevitable when it comes to maintenance, repairs, and upgrades, and has been the demise of many family budgets. Dropping a boat off at the shop can be an agonizing and uncertain time. Questions swirl about whether the parts will be in, how many boats are ahead of me, will they forget about me (this happens more often than it should), or even will it be the all-time favorite, "We can't seem to figure out what's causing that."

Time without a boat moves in slow motion and is magnified by a certain increase in reports from friends of the epic bite we are missing while stuck at home. Billboard messages, which had gone unnoticed, jump into the car, reminding you of what you're missing. Fishing reports of the best bite in a decade abound. All of a sudden, the thousand-dollar repair bill starts to taste a little less bitter when the call comes in to "Come get it, you're ready to fish," until, hilariously at the same time, the reports come in from all angles that the fish "just shut off!"

"FEELING SICK."

There's very little that can keep us from a day out on the water, pursuing the most noble of endeavors: reeling in a bunch of gamefish. Early mornings, crowded fishing holes, bad weather; you name it, we're (mostly) there for it in all kinds of less-than-ideal conditions. But what happens when your stomach is churning and your barking drawers become a scorched skid mark that may get worse? We say, "Suck it up and get after it!"

You might as well try to take your mind off your aches and pains by fighting a rather feisty tuna. There is, however, an upside to not feeling 100 percent. You guessed it . . . use it to your benefit. If you come home with nothing to show for your efforts except a sheepish smile, feel free to say, "How could I possibly focus on the fish when I'm feeling this miserable?"

Did You Know?

The largest fish ever recorded in history was the Leedsichthys, an extinct species that lived during the Jurassic Period and could grow up to an incredible fifty feet in length.

"THERE WAS TOO MUCH SNOW-MELT."

Sure, some diehard anglers fish all year long. However, most fishermen pine away during the cold winter months, waiting for that taste of warm spring air before heading back to the water. As most seasoned anglers know, melting snow can be a problem. Not only can snowmelt rapidly lower the water temperature, but it can also change the pH of the water. Believe it or not, if the water cools off quickly enough, it can actually cause stress in the fish, which can lead to a lack of feeding and even death. If mother nature throws you this curve ball, and you end up with nothing to show for your efforts, you can blame the blizzard last week.

"It's Football Season!"

There isn't much that we'd rather do on a beautiful summer day than go out on the water and try to drown a few worms. But when the first brisk morning fills the air, and the leaves start to think about changing colors, you know what that means . . . FOOTBALL! Whether it's college ball on Saturdays or pro ball on Sundays, you'll find us on our favorite sofas or at our local watering hole rooting on the home teams.

The downside of this American tradition is that it severely cuts into our fishing time. Our solution: Get out on the water earlier and make sure to get home for kickoff. And if the fish aren't biting early in the morning, have no fear: When you get home to your family and friends packed around the big screen, just tell them, "Sure, I could have brought home some big catches, but then I would have missed the game."

"REST IN PEACE—NO ONE IS GETTING OUT OF HERE ALIVE."

We were once out on the water with an older gentleman named Frank. We didn't know Frank well, but after a few hours of casting and catching, we became fast friends. At about midday, he asked if we could steer the boat closer to the nearby road. About fifteen minutes later a funeral procession drove by. Frank took off his hat and lowered his head.

After the cars passed, one of us said, "That was a really nice thing to do." Frank responded with, "It's the least I could do after being married to her for fifteen years." All joking aside, there's very little that can keep us from a date with a reel, rod, and the fish. Yet if you need to cut your day short to attend a most-important event, such as a funeral, at least the upside is you have a built-in excuse . . . "I could have caught more fish but clearly I'm a stand-up person and needed to pay my respects."

"I HAD A WEDDING TO ATTEND."

Okay—we've got another joke for you: An avid fisherman was getting married. The wedding was scheduled at night, so he and his groomsmen decided to hit the lake for a little time with the bass before it was time to get ready. His wife-to-be, who didn't enjoy fishing, told him if he was late to the wedding he might as well not show up at all.

As the hours clicked away, as fate would have it, the groom hooked a big one. While fighting the beast, his best man told him he better cut the line, as it would take too long to reel this one in. And you guessed it, the man said, "It's really a shame because I'm sure she would have made a lovely wife."

So, similar to the "funeral excuse," if you ever walk away the water empty handed, you can always say, "If it wasn't my fiancée's big day, I likely would have had a big day myself."

Did You Know?

The sailfish is the fastest fish in the world, which can swim at speeds of up to 68 miles per hour.

"THERE WERE HUNTERS ON THE LAKE."

The overlap between hunters and anglers is significant. Most hunters fish and most anglers hunt. Many see it as an opportunity to quickly shift with the season to feed their outdoor addiction by putting away their rods and reels and picking up their waders and shotguns. When hunters take it too far is where we must draw the line—they hunt where we fish! Some of our best fishing seasons overlap with duck season and some of our best fishing spots just happen to be prime real estate for the bearded, face painted, and camo'd-up dynasties of the ducks. They arrive hours before sunrise, so we can't beat them. They drag decoys with leaded lines, flapping wings, and spikes into the shallows. Their misbehaved dogs pleasurably swim in a "doggy paddle" motion to ensure any fish alive vacates the area.

"Mr. Mallard, you are in our spot, and we want to fish, so go hunt a deer!"

"Too Many Predators Were Eating the Fish."

Humans have been fishing for about the last forty thousand years. During this time, it is likely that we *Homo sapiens* have been coming up with excuses when we came home empty handed.

Of course, it's not just the hunter-gatherers that have been looking to supplement their diet with aquatic creatures. From cnidarians, octopuses, seals, squid, spiders, cetaceans, grizzly bears, jaguars, wolves, snakes, turtles, and seagulls, many from the animal kingdom have been competing to fill their bellies. Unfortunately, for many hungry anglers, there is a limit to how many fish are in the sea. Yet clearly, if you strike out on the water, an easy excuse is, "This lake is full of predators. I never had a shot."

"MY BEER WAS TOO WARM AND IT THREW OFF MY CONCENTRATION."

Fishing is the best! We love everything about it. From the anticipation of the weekend, the serenity of a beautiful day, and of course, reeling in a big one. So, what can make it even better, you ask? How about a nice frosty beverage on a hot day under the sun? Just thinking about the beads of moisture glistening on the ice-cold bottle makes our mouths water.

But what happens when the day has dragged on, the fish are not cooperating, and the cooler is no longer working efficiently. Say it ain't so! Now you're stuck with a dry throat and a warm beer. The good news is you can use this perilous situation to your advantage. If you happen to come home with nothing to show for your efforts and your buddies are busting your chops, simply ask, "How could I possibly focus on fishing when I was stuck with warm beer?"

"I Let My Buddies Hit All the Good Spots."

Although, at times, we both love going out alone on the water with just the fish and our thoughts, there is something special about sharing the experience with a few of your best friends. The camaraderie of friends joining in the thrill of reeling in a few big ones, sharing a few cool drinks, and some friendly banter can lead to the best of times.

And if you're a really good bud, you'll tip off your compatriots to all your tricks of the trade. You'll show them where to buy the best bait, offer up the right techniques, and, of course, show them where they'll catch the most fish. At the end of the day, if your group has all come back with a boat full of trout, and you have nothing to show for your efforts, just tell your lot, "Sure you caught more fish than me, I gave you the best spots."

"THE LAKE WAS TOO CROWDED."

One of our favorite things about fishing is going out in the early morning or late afternoon, when the water is quiet and still, we are one with nature, and the fish are biting. But we guess it goes without saying that we're not the only ones that enjoy the solo lifestyle. And every angler who has been fishing since they were young has had the experience of going to their secret spot only to find it overpopulated by men and women who have had the same thought.

Quite often catching a lot of fish comes down to simple mathematics. A lot of fish, and very few fishermen, equals a good haul. But when the anglers outnumber the fish, the ratio is sure to work against you. However, do not worry. Because the next time you strike out on the water, just say, "What could I do? The lake was way too crowded."

Did You Know?

There are some species of fish that have the ability to generate electric fields, which they use to navigate and communicate with other fish.

"THE POND IS ALL FISHED OUT."

It's like catching fish in a barrel.

Let us paint a glorious picture. The weather is getting warmer, the days are getting longer, and you decide it's time to dust off the old gear and spend the day at your favorite fishing hole. And lo and behold, the lake has recently been stocked and it feels as if the fish are literally jumping in the boat. Is there anything better?!

But with up comes down, with the good comes the bad, and when word spreads of a fish surplus, an influx of anglers only leads to despair. After several amazing months, you begin to feel a chill in the air, the leaves are changing, and you go out for one last hurrah before hunkering down for the winter. It's back to your lucky spot on your local lake. Yet this time, your fortunes have changed. Not a single bite. As you drive home with your tail between your legs, feel free to tell any of the haters, "There was nothing I could do. The pond was all fished out."

"They Just Weren't Biting Today."

"28-38" was the new nickname for our friend Stan who said they caught a huge 38" grouper, but the next time he told us it was a 28" fish. The next time we talked with him he simply said "They just weren't biting that day." If you've learned anything so far from this book, we hope it's at least the following two pieces of advice: First, a bad day of fishing definitely beats a good day at the office. And secondly, if the fish aren't cooperating it's never, ever your fault. Like "28-38," we all want all of our fishing trips to be great but that just isn't the case.

Poor conditions, other anglers—there is always a valid, or not so valid, reason why you struck out. And on some days, the answer is as simple as rolling out of bed. There are just going to be days when the fish don't do their part. So, the next time your day out at sea doesn't go according to plan, a tried-and-true explanation is as easy as Stan, a.k.a. 28-38 ... "What can I say? The fish just weren't biting today."

"I Hurt My Casting Arm Lifting Weights."

Ok, so you're thirty pounds overweight and on the back nine on the course of life. You haven't worked out in years and couldn't find the gym with a good GPS. But don't let this stop you from a good excuse. As everyone knows—or should know, you've told them countless times—you are an expert angler. You're leaving before dawn and will surely have a bounty of fish by dusk.

You've told your family and friends to come over hungry. But alas, the fish just weren't cooperating. Your famished loved ones begin to grumble quite loudly when you walk through the door empty handed. Not to worry, just look them all square in the eye, flex as much as possible without being overly obvious, and state with full confidence, "I hurt my casting arm doing my last rep of fifty-pound curls and couldn't fish with my normal greatness. So, who wants pizza?"

"I Had a Huge One That Barely Got Away."

For as long as people have been going fishing, there have been dreams about reeling in a huge trophy. And for just as long, anglers have been coming home frustrated, but with a story to tell. Whether the bait fell off the hook, the line snapped, or one of the multitude of other valid reasons your catch squirmed away at the last minute, feel free to use one of the most frequently used excuses known to every fisherman that has ever gone out with aspirations of bringing a feast home to their family or one to mount on the wall, but came home with nothing to show for it. Of course, you know it. Say it with me, "The big one got away!"

"I DIDN'T HAVE MY LUCKY HAT."

To fish well, you need good technique, a lot of knowledge, and of course a little bit of Lady Luck doesn't hurt as well. Sure, you can be well prepared. Of course, you can go to your favorite spot. And perhaps the conditions are prime to catch a boatload of fish as well. Yet, somehow, for reasons that are only known to the great fisherman in the sky, the fish just don't bite. On other days, you can grab some bad bait on a whim, pick up your old pole, and reel 'em in like crazy. Every angler worth their salt knows that as much as you try to predict, this sport can truly be unpredictable. That's why it helps to always keep a little advantage with you. Whether it's the rod that you used to catch a twenty-five-pound trout, or the lure that you used to win a fishing competition, a lucky charm can't hurt. So, the next time you strike and have nothing to show for your efforts, just tell your comrades, "I forgot my lucky hat. I can't catch a thing without it."

"THE RIVER HASN'T BEEN STOCKED THIS YEAR."

You take care of the bait, equipment, and technique, and the environment will take care of the fish. Right? But what if you're fishing in an area without many fishy adversaries, and the water needs to be stocked?

Sure, it can be just as fun to fish a stocked pond, if not more so, than taking your chances in a fully natural setting. If you're in an area that has been filled with carp that are biting like crazy, it can lead to the best of experiences. There is no shame in that. But, what about the alternative? We've all been there—those days when you're having no luck at all. So, if the unthinkable happens, and there just doesn't seem to be anything to catch, just tell anyone who will listen, "Clearly, they haven't stocked the pond yet."

Did You Know?

Clown fish are born male and can change to female
if needed to mate.

"I THINK MY HOOKS WERE TOO DULL."

To catch a lot of fish, you need experience, luck, and to be prepared with the appropriate equipment. However, at the end of the day, if your prey doesn't latch onto your hook, you're out of luck. From bait-cast, fly-cast, and bait and spin-cast lure hooks, there are lots to choose from. And in general, the sharper the better. But why not use this piece of information to your advantage? If you're out for a beautiful day on the water, only to come back frustrated, save some face by saying, "It really wasn't my fault. I think my hooks were just way too dull."

"THE WATER WAS TOO MUDDY."

Whether it's due to the rainy spring weather, snow melt, a river that has a lot of sediment, or a tropical summer system, there are a lot of reasons why the water might be muddy. It doesn't take a rocket scientist to realize that if the water is full of mud, it can be hard for the fish to see. And if the fish can't see the bait, your chances of reeling in a bunch of bass go right down the tubes. Of course, you can try more colorful and/or larger bait, but trust us when we tell you that you're still fighting a murky, underwater battle. On the upside, you have a built-in excuse. If you're out on the water for a fun-filled day, only to be stymied by the conditions, just tell your hungry friends and family, "With muddy conditions like this, it is impossible to catch any fish."

"I HAD AN OFF DAY . . . I'M NORMALLY MUCH BETTER."

This excuse has been used by athletes, businesspeople, lovers, gamblers, students, and generally anyone with a pulse. So, we say, why not use it when the fish don't bite as well? Sure, you are normally the best angler this side of the Mississippi. You can out-fish all your friends, have your name in the paper, and have won contests. You're basically a legend . . . at least in your own mind. But alas, it happens to everyone eventually. Some days the river just doesn't flow, the planets don't align, and the fishing gods conspire against you. Not to worry, just conjure up a look of pure consternation, and say, "I have no idea how this could have happened. I'm normally much better."

"I GOT TO MY FAVORITE SPOT TOO LATE IN THE DAY."

It's a known fact that there are certain areas where fish congregate. And every experienced angler knows precisely where to find the fish biting. Yet, it's also known that fishermen talk. And before you know it, what used to be your hidden gem—your secret spot—can quickly become a destination fishing locale. You've heard it before: "Loose lips sink ships." By the time you get there in the late afternoon, your fellow anglers have been fishing that area all day and have picked up all the big fish.

So, the next time you go to your never-fail sweet spot on your favorite lake, only to find it packed not with fish, but boats and humans, don't despair. In our humble opinion you only have one way to save your reputation. Let everyone who will listen know, "The word is out. My secret spot has been compromised. I'll have to get there earlier tomorrow."

"I Was Trying a New Technique."

Sometimes in life, you need to take a couple of steps back before you can move forward. This is often the case when trying something new. Whether it's trying to learn a new language, a new sport, or just trying a new skill for the first time, it can take several attempts before we see progress. But why not use this to your advantage while out on the water? If you have new bait, are in unknown waters, have changed your gear, or are trying a new technique, and subsequently the fish don't bite like they normally do, just tell your friends, "I was trying something new today. After a few more days of practice, I'm sure I'll have a cooler full of fish."

Did You Know?

The oldest fish ever recorded was an Australian lungfish named Grandma, who lived to be one hundred years old.

"THE FISH ARE FEEDING AT NIGHT."

When the fish are really biting, when it seems like they're jumping out of the water to get the bait, that's when, as an angler, you feel like you are on top of the world. Of course, this glorious feeling obviously requires hungry fish. Unfortunately, a well-fed body of water often leads to apathetic fish. If need be, however, feel free to use this to your advantage. The next time the fish seem to be staring at your bait like a four-year-old looking at a liver dinner, explain it with, "The fish are clearly feeding at night, and we didn't have a chance."

"I Lost My Best Fly on the Stream."

We all have our favorites. Our favorite color, our favorite car, and, when it comes to fishing, our favorite bait. If you ask any angler that's been around the block, they'll surely tell you that different conditions require different approaches. Although, when push comes to shove, almost all fishermen have their go-to necessities to reel in the big one.

But what happens when things go awry? What happens when you're out all day with aspirations of feeding the whole family and only come home with worms? We say take your favorite lure out of your tackle box, find a good hiding space, go home, and simply tell your hungry family, "I lost my best fly on the first cast of the day. It's no wonder I came home with nothing."

"I Didn't Have the Right Lure Color."

The right lure can be an essential part of a productive day. Personally, we like a nice silver lure on bright, sunny days. We've also found that gold lures work well on cloudy, darker days. Using the right lure can be helpful in high or low water, muddy or clear conditions, and the list goes on and on. But this also makes for a perfect excuse. The next time mother nature serves up some interesting conditions, and you come home without any fish, just say, "With these conditions, I really needed a different lure color."

"I RAN OUT OF TIME."

At times, on those glorious days, the fish just seem to jump into the boat. Every time you reel in the line, there seems to be a reward attached to the hook. Yet on other days, no such luck. We've all been there. Sometimes the enemy just isn't biting, and there is nothing to do but to keep trying. Continue to cast, reel, and wait . . . and wait . . . and wait, with the knowledge that eventually, if you wait long enough, you are sure to be rewarded.

But when the sun starts to dip below the horizon, and your stomach is growling with thoughts of dinner waiting at home, it only makes sense to call "mercy." And when you get there, just tell your significant other, "I'm sure I could have caught a few if I just had a little more time."

Did You Know?

Certain fish have been known to use tools to catch their prey. For example, some species of fish use rocks to crack open shells.

"SOMEONE FLIPPED OVER THEIR FISH DURING THE LAST TRIP."

Lady Luck can be a sultry mistress. And if you upset her, it can lead to a very long day. As the Vietnamese will tell you, a surefire way to turn good luck into bad is to flip over a fish and eat the underside of your catch.

If you happen to have a good day on the water, it can be tempting to thumb your nose at the fishing gods. However, you must be careful, or your next time out might be your last. If one of your fishing partners dares to tempt fate leading to a boating disaster the next time out, just explain it with, "My buddy ate the underside of the fish, so our boat was destined to flip."

"I FORGOT TO BRING A COIN TO TOSS INTO THE WATER FOR GOOD LUCK."

Some fishing superstitions go way back. One such belief that has held the test of time is tossing a coin into the water for good luck. The nautical explorers used to do so with the hope that it would ensure a safe passage. Pirates would shell out a little money to assist with a bountiful harvest. This tradition has carried over all the way to the twenty-first century. But if the fish aren't biting, you can always explain it with, "I don't know where my head was, but I forgot to throw a coin into the water before heading out to sea. I, therefore, never had a chance."

"I SKIPPED CHURCH TO FISH AND GOD WAS ANGRY AT ME."

Some days, even if you do everything right, you still come up short. What, ultimately, makes the difference, you may be asking? In our humble opinion, it comes down to the fishing gods. Some days, they're on your side, and on others they seem to put a hex on you. And if you decide to go out early on a Sunday morning, only to come home without a fish, at least you have a built-in excuse: "I skipped church to go fishing and God was clearly angry with me."

"MY BUDDY WASN'T FISHING SERIOUSLY."

Fishing with a friend or two can be so much fun. Everyone working together with one common goal, sharing the experience, can lead to a fun-filled day reeling in one fish after another.

But what happens when your comrades just aren't feeling the energy? Perhaps they're too busy enjoying the weather, or maybe they've been enjoying the beer a bit too much. Regardless, if your fellow anglers aren't focused on the task at hand, it can take down the whole boat . . . so to speak. Therefore, the next time you go out with a couple of your best buddies, only to come home grumpy with a beer buzz and no dinner, explain it with, "My so-called friends weren't taking the challenge seriously. How in the world were we expected to catch any fish?"

"I Couldn't Figure Out What Bait the Fish Were Taking."

As any true angler will tell you, picking the right bait can be the difference between success and failure. Yet, there are so many to choose from. You can use worms, leeches, minnows, crayfish, crickets, and grasshoppers when fishing in freshwater. In saltwater, we reeled in a bunch of fish with sea worms, eels, crabs, shrimp, strips of squid, and cut-up pieces of fish. But even the most experienced fisherman can make a mistake. So, the next time your comrades are snagging one fish after another and you're perpetually recasting, just let them know, "Clearly, I'm using the wrong bait."

Did You Know?

The longest migratory route of any fish is the eel, which travels from Europe to the Sargasso Sea in the Atlantic Ocean to mate and lay eggs.

"GPS Quit Working."

Back to the sundial and compass. We all rely on navigation from GPS-enabled services to get around town, on hikes, and on the water. This handy technology can put anglers on a dime to ensure they are given the opportunity to catch the big one—or a bunch of them. When the GPS is on the brink, we might as well have gone to the baby shower or the dentist. This day is doomed. Some farm pond bassin' or river trout fishin' may get by, but big-water angling on the lake or ocean can quickly turn into an emergency, let alone a no-go for fishing. Fog, wind, darkness, or storms can heavily complicate navigation without GPS. Following your heading on a compass is key for safe navigation back to the dock. GPS is out? We must use the "Go Perfectly Straight" technique to get home.

"My Spouse Said 'Rabbit' Right Before I Went Out."

Whether you're wearing your lucky hat, throwing some salt over your shoulder, or performing a righteous deed for some good karma, sometimes you need a bit of luck on your side. You need to do anything you can to stay away from some bad juju. But did you know that saying certain words can be just as much of a jinx? One such example: never—we mean *never*—use the word "rabbit" while fishing. It's a surefire way to end up with a bad experience. This is likely because of the superstition that the devil may, at times, disguise himself as a rabbit. However, if you do need to explain your woeful performance on the water, you can always say, "My spouse saw a rabbit in our yard and told me all about it right before we went out. We never had a chance!"

"My Buddy Brought a Black Briefcase on Board."

In our opinion, fishing should be mostly about relaxation and having a good time. Leave all of your problems behind, and just let the stress of life melt away. But what happens when one of your fishing buddies is all work and no fun? You know the type.

They just can't fully step away from the office and have to bring some work along. They're constantly answering work calls, emailing the office, and sending out work texts. And the ultimate faux pas is to bring a black briefcase onto the boat. In fishing lore, this means that someone is not coming home. So, the next time your fishing trip doesn't go as planned, just say, "It's bad enough that we didn't catch any fish. I'm just happy with that black briefcase on board that nobody got killed."

"MY SON STEPPED OVER MY RODS."

One of our favorite parts of fishing is passing on the tradition to our children. It brings such happiness to a parent to see the joy on their kids' faces when they reel in their first fish. But, of course, there is a learning curve. Baiting the hook, casting, knowing when to reel in aggressively and when to let out a little line takes practice and persistence. As a parent, you therefore have to be patient with the youngsters when they make a mistake. So, if, for example, your child steps over your rods—which every angler knows is bad luck—you need to be forgiving and use this as a teaching moment for future excursions. There is also another upside: You can still use this to your advantage by stating, "Little Suzie didn't know any better when they stepped over the rods. But at that point we didn't have a chance."

Did You Know?

Contrary to popular belief, there are fish that can survive out of water for extended periods of time— most notably the lungfish, which can breathe air and live out of water for several years.

"Spouse Was Nagging Me to Come Home"

Before many couples meet, occasionally the groom-to-be is a fishing fool. Any free moment is spent fishing in saltwater, freshwater, lakes, oceans, and streams—an unapologetic angler of anything that swims. It was an attractive hobby to her. She also liked to tag along sometimes and catch some rays, and even catch a few fish and there. Seemingly as soon as we started to make plans, the wedding snuck up and blew by, the honeymoon phase was over, and the grind of the growing family was upon us.

There is something about a call from the old lady while on a fishing adventure that tends to ring differently. It is very seldom a "check in on how the fish are biting" or an encouragement to "stay a little longer." The tone, whether spoken words or unspoken, is as clear as a bell with a tinge of "come on home now" or "I thought you would've been home hours ago." With a blessing and a prayer, we can all have spouses who support our attractive hobby well into our wedded years. If you are not in this safe zone, we can't help you. If you are considering lifelong commitment and there is a question in this area, there is a simple test we recommend.

Cast a few lines to test the waters. Some options include suggesting a wedding cake featuring a fishing scene; a fishing-themed wedding for decor and flowers such as lily pad blooms; a husband and wife atop the cake holding fishing rods; fishing boots for shoes or vented shirts for bridesmaids and groomsmen; finally, pitch weaving fishing lyrics into the vows such as, "I thee wed, bass are on the bed."

If your spouse-to-be is reluctant to happily include your fishing passion into the theme of the wedding, then you might be caught in fast-moving waters. But if love prevails, and if you can overcome these differences and tie "the" knot, just know you always have a built-in excuse 'til death do you part: "My spouse was nagging me to come home, so I didn't catch anything."

Did You Know?

In prehistoric times, people would fish with their bare hands. Thankfully, many anglers still partake in this hand-to-gill combat in the form of "noodling" for giant catfish from under rocks, logs, and riverbanks.

"Another Boat Got in My Way."

There are times when having the water to ourselves and enjoying the quiet can feel like a utopia. This scenario is never more prevalent and desirable than when another fisherman gets in our way. It can just be so frustrating when you know exactly where the fish are biting, only to have three other anglers hovering over the area, and consequently, you can't even get a sniff. Or when a guy zooms past your boat at 50 mph, leaving a wake of destruction for your otherwise serene stillness and effectively decreasing your chances for a catch. If you find yourself in a similar situation, how about saying, "I would have had a great day, if those four other boats hadn't been in the way."

"My Spouse Completely Jinxed Me By Wishing Me Good Luck and Telling Me to 'Catch a Lot of Fish.'"

In any good marriage, it helps to have a supportive spouse. A mere "Good luck on your presentation at work," or "Thank you for helping out with the kids" can go a long way. In our opinion, supporting each other is the foundation for a solid relationship. Yet could there be times when a kind word or seemingly helpful gesture can backfire?

As any experienced angler can attest, the answer is a definite "Yes!" While it's great if your better half supports your fishing passion, the last thing you want him or her to do is jinx your mission. For example, if your partner unknowingly offers support, it can lead to a hex. But if the unthinkable happens, and you end up with nothing to show for your efforts, you've got your way out courtesy of your Number One. "My spouse completely jinxed me when they told me to catch a lot of fish."

Epilogue

Most likely, if you've read this book, you love to fish. And we totally get it! The thrill of being out on the water, relishing in the battle, and being rewarded with a large trophy suitable to hang on your wall—is there anything better? If you enjoy fishing as much as us, surely you've been at it enough times to know that not every adventure ends in pay dirt. What about those days when nothing seems to go right? You're burning in the sun, your patience has run thin, and worst of all, you've got to go home and face the music with nothing in your cooler but warm beer. Well, now you have the solution. Keep your chin up, look your naysayers directly in the eye, and pull this little gem off the shelf. Surely, you can find just the right tale with *Fishing's Best Excuses.*

About the Authors

Joshua Shifrin is a licensed psychologist and the author of seventeen books (eighteen, if you include this one!). He loves to write whenever he can find the time. He lives in New Jersey with his beautiful wife and two terrific boys.

Matt Mitchell is a software sales executive, author, and an avid angler. Matt enjoys fishing with family and friends, especially with his wife and teenage daughter, along the "Forgotten Coast" of Florida. An entrepreneur at heart, Matt has invented fishing products and outdoor clothing brands which celebrate the beauty of all things outdoors.